P9-AOF-195

My World

Seasons

by Tammy J. Schlepp

Copper Beech Books
Brookfield, Connecticut

Contents

© Aladdin Books Ltd 2000

Designed and produced by
Aladdin Books Ltd
28 Percy Street
London
W1P 0LD

*First published in the
United States in 2000 by*
Copper Beech Books,
an imprint of
The Millbrook Press
2 Old New Milford Road
Brookfield, Connecticut 06804

Printed in Belgium
All rights reserved

Coordinator
Jim Pipe

Design
Flick, Book Design and Graphics

Picture Research
Brian Hunter Smart

Library of Congress Cataloging-in-Publication Data
Schlepp, Tammy J.
  Seasons/Tammy J. Schlepp.
   p. cm. -- (My world)
  ISBN 0-7613-1224-2 (lib. bdg.) ; 0-7613-2332-5 (paper ed.)
  1. Seasons--Juvenile literature. [1. Seasons.] I. Title. II. My world (Brookfield, Conn.)
QB637.4.S35 2000
508.2--dc21   *8676*   00-055575

Come one! Come all!

Let's meet the seasons.

Hello, rainy spring and sunny summer.

Hi, cool autumn and cold winter.

Do you have a favorite season?

Turn the page to choose.

Boats in summer

Did you know when it's summer
where you are, it's winter
somewhere else in the world?

Did you know the sun shines longer in
summer than in winter?
It's summer! Let's go for a sailboat ride!

4

Did you know that each season is three months long?

Did you know that the shortest day of the year is in winter?
It's winter! Let's build a snowman!

Winter snow

6

How can you tell when it's spring?

Little buds grow on the trees.

Soon the buds blossom
into flowers.

Apple
blossom

Spring

How can you tell when it's spring?

Rain! Rain! Rain!

Spring rain

Meadows turn green and days

grow warmer.

Umbrellas

In the spring you will need your umbrella. Or you'll get wet, wet, wet!

9

How can you tell that it's spring?

You can see the farmer planting seeds.

The seed grows roots in the ground, and

a plant shoot grows toward the sky.

Plowing

Seeds grow

In spring, baby animals are born.

Chirp! Chirp! Chirp!

Do you hear the baby birds

calling to be fed?

Baby birds

How can you tell when it's summer? Look at the fields of flowers. Look at the trees heavy with green leaves. Look at the fruit growing on the branches.

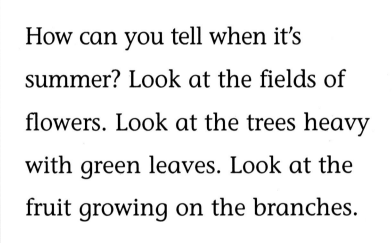

Little apples

Summer flowers

At the beach

How can you tell when it's summer?

The days are long and sunny.

Let's play outside! Let's go to the beach!

All this fun can make you hungry.

Let's have a summer picnic!

In the country

Bee

Butterfly

In summer the grass grows tall and thick. Beautiful butterflies flutter from flower to flower.

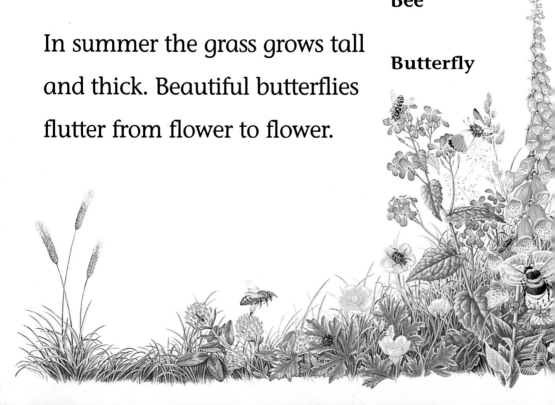

Rabbit

Bees buzz, and the cricket says,
"Chirrup! Chirrup!"

Animals are all about. Do you see that rabbit
munching on green grass?

18

How can you tell when
it's autumn?

Your mother says, "Put on your
jacket. It's cool outside!"

Days are growing shorter, and
brightly colored leaves are falling
to the ground.

Ripe apples

**Autumn
leaves**

Collecting grapes

How can you tell when it's autumn?
You can see the farmers hard at work.

All their crops and fruit are ripe. The
grapes are purple and ready for eating.

Animals are hard at work, too. They know cold weather is on its way, and food will be hard to find.

Squirrel

See the squirrel gathering nuts.
See the birds stuffing themselves on berries.

Blackbird eating berries

How can you tell when it's winter?
Brrr! It's cold! The trees have lost
their leaves. The green grass is gone.
Snow may soon be falling.

Bare branch

Winter trees

Sunny winter days are fun!

An icicle is like a magic wand.

But if you drop it, it will break.

Icicles

Hare

Some animals, like this mouse, go to sleep for the winter. It's called hibernation.

Mouse

Some animals change color. A hare may be white in winter, like the snow. In summer, it is brown like the forest floor.

In a rain forest there are only two seasons.

In the rainy season it rains almost every day.

In the dry season, it rains less often.

Rain forest

South Pole

Desert

In the desert, it is
too dry for most
plants to grow.

In summer at the South Pole,
the sun shines all day and all night.
In winter, the sun never shines.
It is dark and very cold!

Can You Tell?

Can you tell what season it is by looking at plants and animals? Look at these pictures and see.

Blossom

Butterfly

Hare

Ripe apples

Baby bird

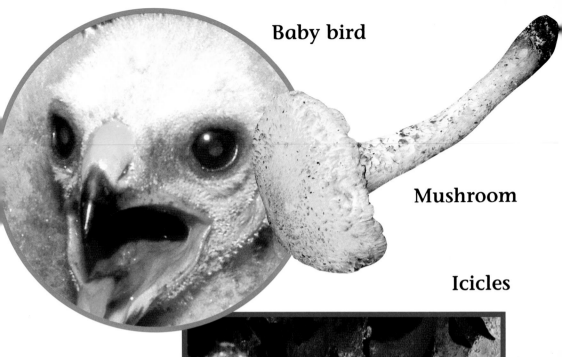

Mushroom

Icicles

Answers on
page 32.

Clue: Look at pages 6, 11,
16, 18, 19, 24, and 25.

Do You Know?

These pictures are of the same place. Can you tell which one shows spring, summer, autumn, or winter?

2

1

The answers
are on
page 32.

3

4

Index

ANSWERS TO QUESTIONS

Page 28-29 – Blossom appears in **spring** • This hare has a white coat in **winter** • You see most butterflies in **summer** • Apples are ripe in **autumn** • Most birds hatch from eggs in **spring** • Most mushrooms appear in **autumn** • Icicles appear on cold **winter** days.

Pages 30-31 – **1** shows the tree in spring • **2** shows the tree in winter • **3** shows the tree in summer **4** shows the tree in autumn.

Photocredits: Abbreviations: t-top, m-middle, b-bottom, r-right, l-left. Cover 1, 3, 8, 12-13, 14, 15, 18-19, 24, 25, 27 both, 28bl, 29tr, 29br—Digital Stock. 4, 16, 20, 26—Corbis Images. 5, 6-7, 9, 22-23, 28ml—Select Pictures. 10, 11, 28mr, 29tl—Stockbyte. 21—John Foxx Images. 30-31 all—Sylvestris/FLPA.
Illustrators: Wayne Ford—Wildlife Art Ltd, Elizabeth Sawyer—SGA.